Let Your Tears Water the Earth

poems by

Gus Speth

www.watershedpublications.org

Let Your Tears Water the Earth
Poems
©2023 Gus Speth

ISBN: 979-8-21831-014-1

Cover art by the author
Design/production, Anne Pace

Printed in the United States
November 2023

This book is available from
Amazon.com, barnesandnoble.com, Ingram,
and indie bookstores across the country
at IndieBound.org

For Cece
a poet in life

Poetry by Gus Speth

What We Have Instead
2019 Shires Press

It's Already Tomorrow
2020 Shires Press

What Will Last
2021 Shires Press

The Blessings
2022 Watershed Publications

A Beach as Long as Life: Complete Poems and Such
2023 www.gusspeth.org/complete-poems

Contents

part two

The Promise

part three

Seriously Funny

What words are these have fall'n from me?
Can calm despair and wild unrest
Be tenants of a single breast,
Or sorrow such a changeling be?

— *Tennyson*

———∽———

Poetry redeems our human possibilities.
Because poetry may provide us with
our best chance to see and embrace the
truth, it is profoundly revolutionary. ...
Poetry says "yes" to the senses, "yes"
to dreaming, "yes" to meaningful work.
Who would not slow down for this?

—*Jim Haba*

part one

Moving on Through Our Lives

Peaches and Cream

One of his earliest memories
the taste of sugar cane.
His dad stripped it with his knife
handed him bite-size pieces.
He chewed the sweet white stalks.
He remembers his father
with admiration, a gentle man,
always telling funny stories.
He is named after his dad.
It was 1946.

He sold elberta peaches to yankees
headed south to Florida on US 301.
The smell of peaches in Carolina heat
and their gentle sweet—irresistible.
He remembers being fired,
but not because he ate too many.
He threw the soft peach at the car
full of unpleasant New Yorkers.
He has no memory of what they had said.
It hit the car's back window right
above that orange Empire State plate.
Mr. Brickle ran out of the filling station,
shouting to head off another Civil War.

He remembers his neighbor,
a rotund Mr. Mutch he called Very,
who had a bakery in town
making delicious French apple pies,
the ones with icing and raisins.
His mother saw how seriously
he devoured them, so she
bought him a regular supply.
He would eat a whole pie
after football practice.
A skinny sophomore, he
aimed for big and strong.
The first-string line he confronted
scrimmaging averaged over 210.
Mr. Mutch's pies could do it,
he was sure.

In New York with his girl Miss C,
they stayed with family friends, Gin and A,
and twice went out to the World's Fair.
A corndog there smothered with
the Chinese mustard sitting innocently nearby
blew a hole through the top of his head
and led to a lifelong addiction
now slaked with excesses of wasabi.
Gin made dinner for them that night
and served his first and best crème brûlée.
He tastes it still, now his favorite dessert,
the hot, crusty top
the cool, smooth bottom.

After college, he and Miss C married.
Then off to England for an extra degree.
In the Scottish Highlands,
his thesis finished, he stumbled
on human remains
atop a heather-covered hill.
Leading the constable back up,
an officer mumbled,
"It takes one damn fool to find another."
Reckoning the innkeeper did it,
promptly descending the Highlands
down to the pleasant banks of the River Tweed,
they bought a well-deserved
Selkirk Bannock and relaxed,
nibbling its deliciousness and inhaling
the cool, clean breeze from the river.

A new Little Miss C was born in 1969,
her first home a cabin on the
shore of lovely Lake Quonnipaug.
It was one of Sarah Jennings' cabins with
her rule of no children. But
holding Little Miss C that first time
strict Sarah melted like an ice cream cone.
A new dad learned that spring
one of life's great thrills,
a sleeping baby on your chest
with the sweet smell of the baby's head
filling you up.

Small Waves Putter About

The tide is out and the small waves putter about.
The beach stretches away as long as life.
Fragments of great shells gather in random piles.
Gray ocean, gray sky, shades of gray today.

The beach stretches away as long as life.
A dot of red in the sand, a child's lost shoe.
Gray ocean, gray sky, shades of gray today.
Is this the way, in all these shades of gray?

A dot of red in the sand, a child's lost shoe.
There was a child once with a bright blue bucket.
Is this the way, in all these shades of gray?
Was he the child and the sand flakes of gold?

There was a child once with a bright blue bucket.
A shimmering beach the day he fell for her forever.
Was he the child and the sand flakes of gold?
Her amber skin glowed in the noon high sun.

A shimmering beach the day he fell for her forever.
The tide was out and the small waves puttered about.
Fragments of great shells were glistening in the sand.
The beach stretches away as long as life.

Old Man Walk

He was bored with the walk to the mailbox.
It was a half mile down the old dirt road
across the field, over the hills and through the woods
to where the town road ended at the neighbor's farm.
Trudge, trudge, once again now almost every day for 15 years.
But it had to be done. Otherwise, the box would fill up,
mostly with catalogues. They were the sheerest junk,
except for the keeper from Victoria's Secret.

High summer and he noticed that the goldenrod was out.
The rain had been incessant; the field had never been so lush.
Queen Anne's Lace floated like little clouds above the grasses.
He could not get the silly dogs to stop eating half-ripe berries.
He shouted obscenities at them, to no avail, and plodded on.
It made him mad that he had seen no Monarchs this year,
maybe one, despite the most luxuriant milkweed.
He read about a tribe of Monarchs in South Carolina.
They stayed put, refusing to migrate,
like those Canada Geese in New Jersey.
Given what was going on, not a bad idea. Stay put.

In the woods, the maple and ash and moosewood
dripped the easy morning rain on him.
In his memory, they had never stayed so green so late.
The ash leaves come late and go early.
He wondered what the ash borers would do to his trees.
He saw a row of tiny red mushrooms
marching across a water-soaked log, and over in the woods
he could see a patch of yellow chanterelles.
He should gather them—
if his legs worked still or they were closer to the road.

He finally reached the mailbox, looked around at the farm.
It always seemed the same.
The three miniature cows looked just like cows, only pint sized.
They were damn pretty. Dusty the donkey was there as usual.
Try as folks might there was simply no way
to reduce the cry of a donkey to letters. A "bray"? Ha!
Dusty's was remarkable, a thing of beauty heard for a mile.
The chickens came out of the barn. The flock seemed bigger.
He'd soon get a dozen of their fine products from the farmer.
He wondered if he should buy some pullets.
Maybe it was time to have laying hens again.
Weirdly, one sounded like a rooster.
Maybe it was. Not a bad life, roostering.
He noticed that the spring lambs, a white and two blacks,
had grown to look like their moms, about the same size.
The dogs taunted them, as they always did, but
they just kept nibbling the abundant greens, oblivious.
He wondered what the farmer had planned for them.

There wasn't much to the mail.
He recalled the cartoon of a Vermont geezer
who'd run a shunt from the mail slot in his door
straight to his pot-bellied stove.
He thought, I am the mailman, slow but sure,
and if I take enough steps, I will be home eventually.
Moseying on, he would see the same things, mostly.
He tried to reassure himself that the little eejits
that had found him were gnats, not blackflies.
The burdock now looked like little purple thistle flowers.
He knew that one day in the fall they would
cover the dogs with abundant sticker seeds.
He spotted a pile of black bear poop
still shiny and as big as a cow paddy.
He wondered how he had missed it earlier
and whether it was the same bear as before.
In the field again, he paused to look south,
over the nearby hills to the magnificent Ascutney
outlined faintly there, a darker shade of blue.
He thought that if he had to walk up and down hills
for a mile every day, it might as well be here.
Not a bad spot.

He turned back to the road
and was surprised he was almost home.

A Long Journey

The last time he put on shoes
he wore a hospital gown.
He took the hall elevator down
and walked out to the street
into a bright early fall sun.
He got some stale cashews
at the Dollar Tree, and
he ate them as he went
across a bridge of sighs.
On the other side, he found
a familiar mossy street
with its canopy of big live oaks
more ancient even than he.
Shuffling along the shade
he passed the skating rink,
the town baseball field,
his dad's old repair shop.
It was a journey, but then
at the county fairgrounds he
saw the Ferris wheel turning.
He went right to the booth
where his high school class was
selling Earl Dukes barbeque
to fairgoers enjoying themselves.
She was working at the booth
and she smiled, and he sat there
at the counter a very long time.

It's Complicated

draining family cookouts
a new chill in the breeze
awkward zoom conversations
the softest Vermont cheese
very late squash in the garden
impossibly golden trees
vacationing from the news
snowless for the skis
a long sad book to read
the kids' spot-on tease
playful ducks to be slaughtered
some memories bring unease
it's sunny and no rain
poison keeps away dog fleas
a limb blocks the plowed road
church service on Christmas Eve
dog-gnawed oriental rug
bracing cold then a sneeze
taking a fall in the forest
so many to try to please
a hard winter kills the ticks
not everyone here agrees

In My Mountain Town

I come from a very small town,
where folks rarely pulled a frown.

A good place with many farmers,
with me one of the rare departures.

Now I'm in these big hills,
a town once again with no frills.

I've spent my life in leveland.
Am I here by mistake, or plan?

Well, I'm here for the community—
for neighbors without ambiguity.

Folks here remind me of my home,
like it's the very same genome.

Real people with people strengths,
knitted together with loving links.

We must hold tight to what we've got!
It is not perfect but it is a lot.

Mainly, we have got each other
(and then sometimes great snow cover).

Whether born here or from afar,
everybody is a rock star.

We Have Rules!

Have our dogs forgiven us for
the rule about the brand-new couch,
their older brother being gone,
the scary noises from the storms,
the treats we do not give,
the cold, cold water from the hose
splashing on their face and nose,
the sometime sharp scolding
for chewing on the molding?

Who am I to know the dogs' minds!

But this I know: despite it all,
they love to walk with us, and if
walking we trip and fall,
they are quick to our side
licking us as we sprawl.
They both greet us each day
with grins and happy words, unsaid
plainly saying we want to play.
They love to snuggle in our bed;
we let them hop up and just lay.
Should there be a new rule instead?

Friendship

She was an old dog,
hard of seeing, hearing,
and an awful winter:
snow rain melt freeze,
snow rain melt freeze—
everything slick with ice.
The old man let her out
to do her business.
He saw her standing
at the edge of the yard,
the big hill dropping
fast down to the woods,
a steep sledding slope
for the grandkids.

A glance later she was gone.
One step too far, with
ancient limbs and no traction,
she had slid away.

He dressed hurriedly
and spotted her trapped
in a jumble of bramble
down at the bottom,
occasionally struggling
but with no effect.
The old man's back was afflicted,
painful and giving out.
Still he headed down,
stumbling to the bottom.

The dog seemed glad
to have him by her side.
He was glad to be there too.
He lifted her big Lab body
and started up the hill.
When the pain was too great,
he paused, let it subside,
remembered she had been
an acrobat at Frisbee, had
loved to play with the ducks.

He thought: two elder residents
of town in trouble and now
struggling together to get
up a hill covered with ice.
What could be better?

He lifted her one last time
as they approached the stone steps
to the house, and it was too much.
His feet slipped out from under him,
the dog let loose as he reached for the ice.
His head landed inches from the steps.
He rolled over, looked up, and grinned
as she stood licking his face.

Something Happened, She Said

I can't remember tomorrow.
It was just yesterday that
I could remember it well.
But today happened.
First there was a message
and then we got the news,
and the future went away.

Unsung Heroes

scarves
grammarians
pallets
Neosporin
accountants
extension cords
Mexican workers
baking soda
technical colleges
handrails
conjunctions
lacrosse
nurses
U.S. Army-Navy Hymnal
glass panes
acrylic paint
spiders
The United Nations
repair shops
sociologists
water hoses
Medicaid
soy sauce
credit unions
librarians

Passing Days

A hundred Black Skimmers swirl above the inlet.
First signs of a lovely day.

We walked on the beach this morning.
She gave me a surprise kiss.

If only dogs knew their birthdays,
there would be so many more parties.

The year of the rabbit begins today.
I will hop to, for there is much still to do.

That day I turned 81 I applied for the sales job
at Bits of Lace.

Remote from remotes, no devices except my own.
A lovely day in the past.

One day I said, please bare with me,
and she did.

We say today is the day,
but there is always mañana.

The Smile

An artist sketched her, using freestyle.
He got it right— she was all smile.

She has that smile, reaches my heart.
She is at peace. It makes me part.

Pulled over once, she melted the cop.
He said to her, I regret the stop.

Maybe eyes too, but I am sure,
the soul's window: her smile's allure.

It is my cure when I am down.
I look round 'til that smile is found.

Things Are Closer Than They Appear

She said one day she was ready to go.
Go to where, I try not to think I know.
She had bought us a cemetery plot
on a hillside spot that she liked a lot.
It is lovely there, covered now in snow.

I have to think further on this matter.
At first my thoughts made me sadder.
Are things really coming to an end
for me and for my sweet best friend?
Are we soon to climb Jacob's Ladder?

Of course, she meant she was prepared
for the ending that no one's spared.
Her words had shattered my easy day,
raising new things for me to weigh.
She had told me because she cared.

So, problems wait around the door,
ones we can no longer ignore.
But we will go on undeterred
by a future inevitably blurred.
There is so much left to explore.

Zombies Walking

Her slip's showing.
Math's beyond her knowing.
Make a carbon copy.
His handwriting's sloppy.
The check is in the mail.
That's beyond the pale.
He's seated below the salt.
The misbehavior's his own fault.
Sunday is a day of rest.
You must wear your Sunday best.
The iceman comes.
The Colorado runs.
It's a free market.
You can bank on it.
It's a shotgun wedding.
It's good sledding.
Let's go out to the movie.
His flattop's groovy.
Justice is blind.
Make payment in kind.
The woods go on forever.
Humans are very clever.
Ease off the gas pedal.
The loser also gets a medal.

Those of a Certain Age

Will you please run ahead and see
what's around the corner for me?
I think I know what's in my book,
but I need you to take a look.

There is an end for me out there.
A peaceful one you see, my dear?
Or will there be a drug-soaked pain,
and you wishing me gone in vain?

I hope it's sudden, in my sleep,
with no more promises for me to keep.
I don't know how brave I would be
facing out to that endless sea.

I'll remember what our child said
about the truth of being dead.
She said it is okay to mourn
but death is like before you're born.

Threads in the Tapestry

He saw it coming,
saw the wreckage coming,
wreckage driven ever on
and on by the warming,
the rising, and the changing.
Saw it early, decades ago,
and he cried out,
thinking they would listen.
He saw then that it was
the heart that would decide.
He cried to a big world
from a small pulpit.

Young then and hopeful,
hopeful that words would matter,
words could reach the heart.
And so he wrote, invoking
the whole life community
that evolved here with us—
life we did not create and
over which we are not lord.

Years later, as an old man,
he challenged his few readers
to imagine Earth without us.
When asked why he would
even think such a thing, he said,
consider the wreckage
gathering at your feet.
Does it not break your heart?

Now pause, he said, be still,
and contemplate such a world:
living canopies so vast
a small squirrel can move in trees
from the Delaware to the Mississippi,
oceans so fish-filled there appear
to be paths across the water,
flocks of passenger pigeons that
cast large shadows on the landscape,
great herds of ungulates
grazing across cool savannahs,
an Earth thriving with diversity.

But without us.
It's a test, he said, of our
environmental imagination.
If we can imagine such a world
with feelings of awe and reverence,
taking joy in its existence
even though we are no part of it,
nature for nature's sake,
then we are ready
to answer a question.

What is a species worth?
Perhaps just a small part
of nature's tapestry?
It depends on what is
vital and alive to you,
what your imagination sees.
Place yourself, the old man urged,
not as superior to nature
but as evolution's child,
close kin to wild things,
part of nature's flourishing,
threads in the tapestry.
Then you will know the answer.
The heart will decide.

Giving Out

It is strange what is happening to me.
As I am finishing up here on Earth,
I find that I want to share pieces
of me, until there is nothing left.
I won't be happy until I am all gone.

Here, take my library, good books
collected over a lifetime of trying.
And these paintings, I will write your
name on the back of the ones you want.
This house is willed to you, if you
promise to care for the dogs.
Do you need someone to review your draft?
Or some advice or a contact or reference?
Or someone to show up at your event? Gladly,
I give you a piece of my time remaining.

Most important of what I have to give,
I think, are the things I have written, and
the ideas that reappear there stubbornly.
Giving them up is too easy since
they were always made to share
and they are never gone away.
Some gift! Given but not.
It is embarrassing to share them
with friends who have not asked.
An old man clinging to relevance,
or a kid who has seen a bit of light?
I am hardly the best to judge.

The last thing I will give will be
some nourishment back to Earth.
Every extra little bit will be needed.

The Man with a Farm

An old man lives up a hillside
on a rundown farmstead
not close to the center of town.
His unpainted house needs repair;
rusting machinery is scattered about.
He stays in one small room downstairs.
Folks bring to him baskets of food
at Christmas and at Thanksgiving,
but he is easy to forget—
alone, a distance from neighbors.
He has no kin; he has no dog.
He can move only with difficulty.
Trash piles up in the room.
The end of his belt hangs over
a foot below his now-thin waist.
He forgets about zipping his pants.

Do we know what keeps him going?
Does he think about his mother?
Does he carry memories of the farm
as it once was with milking cows
and his wife and son helping him
and he is there on the tractor
tedding the hay loudly singing church songs.
Does he love the lilacs now flourishing
in the rich soil around the falling barn?

As he struggles to make another day,
does he think this is just the way?
Some say that may be best for him.
Yet he may wish a better end.
He may like to see his land alive again,
long for someone to help him in his tub.
He may think there should be friends.

Old Legs

These old legs don't like stairs anymore
or steep slopes or rocks or roots.
But I will accept this and be thankful.
Once they could jump to touch the rim
and pull out down the line to trap block
and kneel at the altar near forever
assisting the Reverend with Communion
and carry three children up Jack Mountain
and kick the mile-long swim needed to be lifeguard.
Now their gift is the stiff walk of an old man
and a shuffling and out-of-balance gait.
But how can I blame them?
They screed straight-down slopes in the Rockies.
They suffered sprains and scrapes and dog bites
and being ripped wide open by a cleat.
They stood there for countless hours
at soccer games, receptions, and speeches
and had no real complaint to offer.
On a special day in 1965 they did their job:
despite a case of nerves and trembling,
they faked a steady walk down the aisle.
The doctor said bodies are made to move.
Me and my old legs will keep on walking.

part two

The Promise

Bread and Roses

When the big sea has stopped rising
and the maps we're through revising
and I can think of storms as friends,
I'll go down to the beach again.

I'll stand still there in that bright surf
and sing a song to this dear Earth.
I'll sing for climate change to end.
I'll sing tears for where we have been.

I'll sing to things that we have learned—
the fossils we should not have burned
releasing the power of former suns,
bringing losses that cannot be undone.

Sad losses the children will inherit.
Species gone without much credit,
thanks to the piles of money earned
and all the corners left unturned.

I'll sing to anger rising still.
Our leaders let firms do their will.
The people did assert control
but not before the barons stole.

Our job is now to make the best,
finding purpose in what is left.
It is a joy to live to fight
and on that beach to fly two kites.

We, The People

If we could restart the US of A,
where then would we begin
to give the clock new spin
and take the role creators play?

We will mainly focus on the Founders
and their badly flawed creation,
the much-revered Constitution.
On it the country nearly founders.

To start, there will be no first sin.
Humans will not be slaves.
Our story better then behaves,
so much evil gone with the wind.

Our democracy very nearly dies
when states not people vote.
It's time for us to now demote
the not-so-great Great Compromise.

The Electoral College must also go.
The popular vote is ignored.
The People once again get gored.
To that, our new democracy says no.

All this is made worse when corporations
are "people" and their money "speech."
They now have extraordinary reach,
matching the power of ordinary nations.

The Commerce Clause must be rethought.
It can block community action
and easily undermine local traction.
Our priority cannot be to have things bought.

It is odd that states control elections.
The foundation of national government
easily shaken by corrupt state ferment.
We'll make a new deal for voters' selections.

We will enshrine the right to privacy,
making it explicit in our new document.
There, it would be the Choice complement
to all the other rights we see.

The right of individuals to carry a gun
wasn't there, until in 2008 the Court said yes.
We will reclaim gun control from this mess
and return our streets to having fun.

We humans invented having rights,
but gave them all to ourselves.
Omitting "rights of nature" compels
action to correct the oversight.

We know we can't start America again.
It is a day dream that comes to this end.
But there is much that we can mend
if together we make history bend.

For our democracy's shortfalls
there are now work arounds.
We can get to better ground,
bursting new and ancient walls.

Government of, by, and for the people,
that is the essence of democracy,
the meaning of popular sovereignty,
the bright light in the steeple.

Tale of a Small Planet

Perhaps the whole root of our trouble, the human
trouble, is that we will sacrifice all the beauty of our
lives, will imprison ourselves in totems, taboos, crosses,
blood sacrifices, steeples, mosques, races, armies, flags,
nations, in order to deny the fact of death.

— James Baldwin, *The Fire Next Time*

Somehow,
in the staggering vastness of the universe,
a small but glorious ball of life was born.
As its eons passed,
a myriad of extraordinary life forms evolved there.
Among them was the species homo sapiens,
a small bipedal mammal distinguished initially
for its very big brain, which helped it to flourish.
Those with big brains, the human beings,
grew in time to love music and art and
found special pleasure in story-telling and gift-giving.
Partly because they evolved as integral to it,
partly because it sustained them in many ways,
the life-giving world around them was revered.
They found it beautiful and were inspired.

But,
as those big brains grew stronger,
an extraordinary, world-shattering thing had happened.
Humans began to reflect on their own existence,
to be aware of themselves as alive individuals,
to know their own reflections in a pool,
and so also to contemplate their own deaths.

Animals all fight or flee when threatened, but
the powerful human desire and consuming drive
to deny and transcend their own oncoming deaths
was something altogether different,
something utterly new to the world.
Quickly, the remarkable power of the big brain
was harnessed to this uniquely human struggle
and things began to happen.

So,
as millennia came and went,
humans pursued several ways to cope
with the devastating realization,
the reality of their own mortality.
Most common has been belief in an Afterlife.
Another has been belief in Reincarnation.
An extraordinary approach has been to create
something that continues to exist after death,
perhaps a giant stone memorial or a small poem.
Perhaps a family, or even a family name, or a farm.
Or something for the history books. Perhaps an empire.
Something that says, very quietly or quite loudly:
"I was here. Don't forget me."

Meanwhile,
a development more indirect and more devastating
was occurring in many ways and places.
Faced with their vulnerability and ephemerality,
humans have also compensated for their fatal weakness
with striving to become grand and invulnerable.

They have done this by gathering and by growing
wealth and status and power. To aid this approach
to coping with existential angst,
certain economic arrangements have been preferred.
These arrangements have, by design,
provided full opportunity for:
possession and control,
growth and expansion,
dominion and extraction,
public recognition and preeminence.

And,
allowing, even favoring competition
in these evolving economic systems
has unleashed a more powerful dynamics
involving insatiable accumulation and growth,
ruthless exploitation of people and natural resources,
and vast inequalities of wealth and power.

Here we are.
It has been asked, only somewhat in jest,
whether the big brain was actually a good idea.
It has also been asked what is to be done now?
The answer, it would seem, is to be found
in this little tale of a lovely planet and its inhabitants.

Heretical, Cynical, or True?

That government which governs least governs ... poorly.

Government interference in the economy is ... necessary.

Economic freedom is the path to riches ... for the few.

America is the land of equal opportunity ... for fast food wages.

People get what they deserve ... in the afterlife.

Democracy is the best form of government ... if only we had it.

Corporate responsibility is ... an oxymoron.

The important things in life ... aren't things.

The more you buy, the happier you ... are not.

Green consumerism is ... still consumerism.

The future is unknowable ... if you don't think.

Things are getting better ... after they finish getting worse.

High Tide

It did not used to be this way.
High tide is now at our front door.
It seems to get worse every day.
God must not like us anymore.

High tide is now at our front door.
The rains have drowned the roads in mud.
God must not like us anymore.
Climate change is God's new Flood.

The rains have drowned the roads in mud.
The oceans are too hot for fish.
Climate change is God's new Flood.
It will not do to sit and wish.

The oceans are too hot for fish.
Our kids' lives are what is at stake.
It will not do to sit and wish.
What strong action must we now take?

Our kids' lives are what is at stake.
It's time to close the fossil beast.
That strong action we must now take.
It's time to stop their deadly feast.

It is time to close the fossil beast.
Our Ark must be disruptive action.
It's time to stop their deadly feast.
Making them pay is just exaction.

Our Ark must be disruptive action.
It seems to get worse every day.
Making them pay is just exaction.
It did not used to be this way.

State of the Union

We so want America to succeed!
But the struggle is uphill, steeply.
The economic system is hard wired
for production and profit and power,
not for people and place and planet.
A fabled Constitution is outmoded,
its many checks and balances instead
saddling us with clogs and barriers,
while repeatedly providing against
government of, by, and for the people.

And if that were not enough,
now, just when a new sense
of national purpose is imperative,
when concerted action is most demanded,
the people themselves are cleaved,
in trenches facing each other in mutual rejection,
with massive efforts expended
for small gains, often rolled back.
We now know much about the divide
and the major role of racism fueling it.

It is hard to see where to turn!
The books are full of good proposals,
both reformist and radical,
for near-term and long.
We know what must be done.
But how? That is the question.

This we can do.
We can search for small openings
seizing opportunities wherever.
We can be crisis ready, anticipating
moments of punctuated equilibrium
when impossible becomes inevitable.
We can back leaders with vision and skill
in the mold of FDR and LBJ and MLK.
We can meld now-siloed progressive energies
into an unprecedented fusion of forces.
We can sustain journalism and scholarship
to keep truth alive and core values burnished.
We can embrace our preachers and prophets,
those who elevate new values and battered spirits.
We can hold each other tightly.

There are some encouragements and,
even more, avenues for engagement.
Among the building blocks now evident,
labor activism is increasing,
as is activism among the young,
the marginalized, and the victims.
Doubts about current order are surfacing,
and calls for transformative change
grow louder in the country.
Aversion to socialist ideas is fading,
at least for young people.

Recent affirmations of government action
challenge the hold of market fundamentalism.
The rising menace of climate change
is bringing home the imperative of
a strong, effective government
of, by, and for the people.
Federal paralysis is countered partially
by impressive initiatives by states and localities.
The threat to democracy is recognized,
and the fight for a democratic future is joined.

All is not lost, but it is already a close call.

Scary

I'll tote it in my garden
or at the soccer game.
I'll take it to church.
Everywhere's the same.

Guns, guns, guns!
It is my right to carry!
Guns, guns, guns!
I like they make me scary.

I will shoot any moving critter.
Nature is my rifle range.
It is a thrill to see them drop.
No reason for that to change.

My friends ask me why I carry.
I once knew the answer.
Now I say it's for protection.
Damn sight better than a taser.

Sure, there will be mistakes,
like the time I shot the preacher.
Freedom will always have a price.
And I've never shot a teacher.

Guns, guns, guns!
It is my right to carry!
Guns, guns, guns!
I like they make me scary.

The Faithful

They carry on.
They do not care
about the odds.
Perhaps their fight
is now hopeless.
Hope is not part
of their thinking.
They are instead
motivated
by a vision—
something better
now awaiting,
a place of peace,
people laughing,
Earth flourishing.
Their cause is right.
They are faithful
to the struggle.
I will embrace
these my brothers
and my sisters.
They are warriors.

The Fall

The summer had been powerful.
It did not yield easily to the fall.
The trees turned slowly,
each at its own pace.

The fall came around politely.
The woods near the house moved
from green to gold with grace,
giving respect to that lush summer.

Such glory could not last long.
Soon gold leaf was floating down.
Vermont's Great Season would come.
Forests of stick would signal its coming.

Suddenly the woods went quiet.
A hawk was near, on the low branch.
The mighty and the meek,
then sensing each other.

What will become of them—
the seasons, the trees, the birds?
Let your heart beat defiance.
Let your tears water the earth.

The Real Problem

Imagine
every morning when you wake up,
beyond your nice view
and over the horizon,
there are 8 billion people out there.

Imagine
8 billion people
searching every day
food and water
shelter and safety
affection and joy
and, much more complicated,
identity and status,
recognition and self-esteem,
and, oh yes, meaning.

Imagine
our world was once empty—
few people and little human activity.
Now we live in a full world,
brimming over with more activity
than it can handle comfortably.

But consider
even if math is not your thing,
fifteen percent of the world's 8 billion
are blessed to live in the rich countries.
Yet each of us has ten times
the environmental footprint of
a person living in poor countries.
Taken together, the rich fifteen percent
do twice the environmental damage
of the vastly larger poor majority.
No one is innocent.
But some are more guilty than others.

A Prayer

Can I banish despair with hope,
    if hope is paired with action?
Can I find a heaven for dogs,
    for them and those who love them?
Can I understand quantum mechanics,
    at least a smidgen please?
Can I write enough to clear my name,
    purging my mistakes and errors?
Can I stay both alert and anguished
    until I have done all I can?
Can I finally admit there are angels,
    since I have now seen some at work?
Can I cry in front of other people,
    and not just when alone?
Can I have some hugs again,
    free of the damn virus?
Can I find some untapped strength,
    and lighten burdens with it?

A Movement of Movements

In my imagination, the activist communities to which many of us feel close affection are each in separate little boats paddling ourselves through swirling waters. Whether flagged environmental integrity, social and economic justice, community solidarity, or people's democracy, sometimes our boats go forward, then backwards, sometimes sideways. But one cannot help but notice that the boats tend strongly to move together, carried along by currents more powerful than our efforts.

Far too often, progressives neglect the underlying currents that are powerfully affecting all our boats. These currents heavily determine whether we make progress in our journeys or move backwards or go nowhere at all.

To succeed in the major ways we dream about requires understanding those underlying forces that shape our prospects. Once we know what we are dealing with, the good news is that progressives can join together in facing a shared situation. The inconvenient news is that when we look at the common, underlying causes of the problems, we find forces that are often deeply burrowed in the mainstream, often so widely and conventionally accepted that to challenge them appears radical to many.

Any search for the sources of the currents holding back real progress must start with the political and economic system. Its prominent features include ramping up GDP, growing corporate profits, focusing on high financial returns to guide investments, increasing the incomes of the already well-to-do, neglecting those marginalized and desperate, promoting runaway consumerism, facilitating great bastions of corporate political and economic power, and pursuing a host of self-serving and harmful policies internationally—all the while demonizing governmental efforts to correct its side-effects and shortcomings.

There are more sources of unwelcomed currents, of course. Dominant cultural values tend decidedly materialistic and anthropocentric. Democracy is impaired in many countries. And there is an ever-active military-industrial complex working away.

It is hard to see where to turn! We know what must be done. But how? That is the question.

This we can do. We can search for small openings seizing opportunities wherever. We can be crisis ready, anticipating moments of punctuated equilibrium when impossible becomes inevitable. We can back leaders with vision and skill. We can meld now-siloed progressive energies into an unprecedented fusion of forces. We can sustain journalism and scholarship to keep truth alive and core values burnished. We can embrace our preachers and prophets, those who elevate new values and battered spirits. We can hold each other tightly.

There are some encouragements and, even more, avenues for engagement. Among the building blocks now evident, activism is increasing, especially among the young, the marginalized, the victims as well as organized labor. Doubts about current order are surfacing, and calls for transformative change grow louder. Aversion to socialist ideas is fading where they were once off-limits, especially for young people. The rising menace of climate change is bringing home the imperative of a strong, effective government of, by, and for the people. The threat to democracy is recognized, and the fight for a democratic future is joined.

There are some positive currents driving toward transformative change, and they will likely strengthen in the future. The possibility progressives must face, however, is that this strengthening will be too modest and too slow to head off a series of genuine catastrophes. This possibility underscores the imperative of progressives leaving their own little boats—their issue silos—and together forging a mighty political force for deep, transformative change. This fusion of forces, a movement of movements, would be new and could make all the difference.

Thinking Like a Mountain

Aldo Leopold knew nature
like few before or after.
He urged those who listened
"to think like a mountain."

Well, hell, I say, I am a mountain!
I am Storm King, here beside the Hudson,
a sentinel with which to reckon.

From my shining east flank I
often heard Pete Seeger singing,
notes forming tunes and rising
from the bow of the sloop Clearwater
as it tacked the Highland's wind gate.
From far on my top I've seen
many times, way past when,
Clearwater and Pete were strongest
sailing upstream against the wind.

Pete sang to all the parts of me,
not just my verdant slopes rising steep
from the fast-flowing river, but the parts that
move around, rub brown fur against
the parts that sink deep in me and share
my waters and my nourishment.
I give it freely, as do critters too small to see.
They too are part of me.

My leaves shimmer in chartreuse,
for spring I am bringing back.
I want to hear the ovenbird again,
to help the goldfinch find its gold,
to see soon the evening grosbeak
dancing among my limbs and leaves.

If you want to think like a mountain,
you must come to see me whole.
Energy flows coursing through me;
life each day from entropy stole.
Can you come to see me sacred,
all the beauty consecrated?
I am alive and fertile and fecund,
providing sustenance and refuge.

I know then what I am,
what I do in this world,
how to weather many threats,
how yet to sing back to the river,
how I am old, yes also that.
But even now I, Storm King,
am not clear on all that we
mountains are supposed to think.
I have told what Aldo meant.
Perhaps that is enough.
But there may be other thoughts,
thoughts waiting to be remembered.

If I Were a Praying Person

If I were a praying person,
as many praying people do,
I would make a list
of those for whom I pray.

I would pray first for the children
for they are inheriting a most difficult world.

I would pray for the poor and destitute
for despite having little, they persevere.

I would pray for the oppressed minorities
for despite their suffering, they show the way.

I would pray for the living things, small and large,
for their homes are being destroyed.

I would pray for the rich and powerful
for they are the most in need of forgiveness.

I would pray for the teachers
    and the preachers
    and the journalists
    and the scholars
    and the artists
    and the parents
for they must keep both truth and hope alive.

I would pray for the generations ahead
for they must remake the world.

And I would pray for the mothers
for the world is lost without moms.

What We Have Instead

In this our world

If there is meaning
we create it.

If there is community
we build it.

If there is justice
we forge it.

If there is providence
we provide it.

If there is love
we extend it.

Nothing is given
save life itself.

We have only
this speck of earth
and each other.

It is enough.

So let us pray
to fields and friends
and to the spacious sky.

It's Just Another Day in America

No more insurance along the Gulf Coast,
over in Carolina or out West.
The floods and fires are too severe.
It's only the money that makes them care.

There's been a new mass shooting in Florida,
but there is no movement on gun control.
Shootings now one a day it does appear,
taking away good folks that were held dear.

One in ten of us awoke destitute,
facing a day short of money and food.
They say the economy is in high gear;
the money just reaches a thin veneer.

Many states are working to take the vote
from folks who are not old and white like me.
All this I fear could be our New Frontier—
echoes of JFK too far, too faint to hear.

There can be a reckoning at the polls
only if our democracy still holds.
Bad things closer than they appear—
It's our job now to make that clear.

It's just another day in America.

Hug Your Librarian

Without books
there is no education.
Without education
there is no First Amendment.
Without the First Amendment
there is no America.
Without books
free speech is
all sound and fury
signifying nothing.

Next

a new day underway
building in the shadows
just over the horizon
piece by piece
place by place
stunning in what it asks of us
in cities not well known
in churches with half members
in councils long forgotten
in families once apart
in unions nearly crushed
in co-ops gone to seed
we see new life
rising up
up rising

many local initiatives now
coming together as new systems
systems of ownership by workers
of health care and education without division
of needs met without consumerism
of economy without growthmania
of energy without pollution
of reverence for nature's miracle
of commitment to climate's protection
of community and mutual support
of popular sovereignty
yes democracy of, by and for all the people

all the people
  (sharing supporting caring giving loving working creating
  participating debating voting demanding protesting provoking
  listening learning playing worshiping trying crying trying again
  tolerating respecting empathizing honoring)
being people
people of all races and genders and religions
bound together by good laws and good fellowship
by music and laughter.

The Islanders

They settled on an island
far off the coast of Maine.
They came for the clean air
and for the bracing cold,
the breakers on the rocks,
the innocence of birds.

They often came in pairs,
their children gone away.
Some settled by themselves,
their partners then gone too.
They reached out to each other.
And it was enough.

They shared one great thing:
In a hundred different ways
they had fought a good fight.
They had seen the world's beauty
but struggled with its horrors.
And they were chastened.

They celebrated the animals and the plants
and so also St. Francis and Pope Francis,
and were found often in quiet reflection.
They lived there with laughter and song.
They flew flags of rainbow and black
and, yes, of red, white, and blue.

part three

Seriously Funny

Learning About Deaning

I was proud to become a dean.
The provost then had a joke for me.
A rich man came to Yale to see
and for his visit he had a screen.

"I'll meet the president," said he,
"but no one lower than a dean."
"No problem," he was told, "We agree.
There is no one lower than a dean."

You may recall Handsome Dan,
Yale's famous bulldog mascot,
a dog I wish I'd soon forgot.
For Dan, I did what a new dean can.

Dan attended a big reception,
one I had for all our donors.
Dan had fun eating cheese sliders
but upchucked all without exception.

Being dean, I looked around for staff
as the crowd stepped carefully
around what was in Dan's belly
and some guests suppressed a laugh.

Soon I was on my hands and knees
armed with some paper towel
and with a ruler for a trowel,
wondering if it was blue cheese.

So I was off to a very good start!
Being dean requires an attitude
of living through all vicissitudes.
I was learning to play the part.

Our Jack

Through Jack's old brain
the ideas fly,
hardly stopping
to say goodbye.

He has to talk
to a big group.
He wrote his text.
It follows soup.

He wonders did
he brush his teeth.
His teeth feel Yes,
to his relief.

He did his tie.
His shirt was white.
Ready to go!
All seemed alright.

But things came loose.
Jack was midway,
his pages were
in disarray.

He had no choice.
Keep on reading!
No one noticed.
Fears receding.

It was over
in the middle,
and no one cared,
not one piddle.

The crowd it cheered.
They loved old Jack.
He was their man
with no going back.

The Human Condition – Part I

On hot days an old man named Joe
would head to the beach for the show.
The bikinis were getting quite meager
and he would dream of being still eager.
On his trip home he was simply aglow.

∞

George was on the cusp of success.
He gave his big job no rest.
But he lost his family and friends,
and he came soon to doubt his ends.
So he asked Siri what she'd suggest.

∞

There was once a guy named Rice
who wrote poems near the end of his life.
A few said they were good,
but no one really understood:
writing them was his *Dune* spice.

There was a young chap named Nate
who always noted the food on your plate.
His wife warned, "On pain of our sever,
Nate, you must not ever, ever
comment on what a woman ate!"

၈၅

There was a Black man named Strong
who knew he was done wrong.
He was told "just get along"
but he refused that old song
and instead he sued Officer Braun.

Freedom Isn't Free

A prominent man named Panetta
was smitten by the bordello's Loretta.
He loved her dark almond eyes
and adored her marmalade thighs.
But soon he came to regret her.

The police raided the bordello
just as the weed was getting him mellow.
He was completely surprised;
he was found compromised.
His solid respectability could become Jello.

He claimed he was inspecting the place,
said his business needed the space.
Loretta he said was his partner,
that she was the one who was smarter.
He thought that would buy him some grace.

The friendly police let Panetta go free.
But that did not let the matter be.
Loretta was a good business lady
and just a little bit shady.
Each year he pays her a big fee.

Chinese New Year's Resolutions

It is the Year of the Rat.
Be the unbelled cat.

It is the Year of the Ox.
Be strong, a Fort Knox.

It is the Year of the Tiger.
Be fierce, but quieter.

It is the Year of the Rabbit.
Be still, a new habit.

It is the Year of the Dragon.
Be the circle of the wagons.

It is the Year of the Snake.
Be alert and awake.

It is the Year of the Horse.
Be a gentle great force.

It is the Year of the Goat.
Be the butt of a good joke.

It is the Year of the Monkey.
Be clever and spunky.

It is the Year of the Rooster.
Be a morale booster.

It is the Year of the Dog.
Be a friend for the long slog.

It is the Year of the Pig.
Be steady, no zag-zig.

The Human Condition – Part II

Two wives whose lives were on repeat
decided that life without men would be sweet.
They bought themselves a used car
but the car didn't go very far.
So they called a mechanic named Pete.

∽

Teachers of a new poet named Vince
said he should use "the personal intense."
Poems should not be a talk at TED, they said,
or sound like the lectures he once read.
Still, he wrote on matters of social consequence.

∽

What a beautiful bird, the Macaw!
More colorful than what we before saw.
Yet Nature was troubled by such beauty
and saw balancing that beauty her duty.
Macaws now croak the most awful Craw! Craw!

There was a young dog named Sally
who on walks would famously dally.
One day she met Billy the beagle
and off they flew like an eagle.
Now she knows all about phalli.

∾

Some said Darius was stroppy.
They said he was always grumpy.
But what's a person to do?
All his gripes were perfectly true!
His bad attitude just came naturally.

Johnny's Confession

Before the wrong me emerges,
know I resisted half my urges!

The other half? My life's story.
It's a story shorn of glory.

I thought at first my BB sights
could not shoot out the town street lights.[1]

I made the fake IDs, a little gold.
Some friend, the one who told.[2]

Shoplifting then seemed smartest.
Hiding Pringles was the hardest.[3]

I stole some bikes, a mere trifle.
So then I stole a motorcycle.[4]

I took it round the Cabot Trail.
How easily I ended up in jail! [5]

The judge said, "Son, you must reform.
You must obey the common norm." [6]

In back my mom then shouted,
"Make the jail one more crowded!" [7]

My mom had long been worn with me.
Now that was there for all to see.[8]

The judge then said, "He's just like boys.
It is your mind with which he toys." [9]

So, I own up to all the things I've done.
I was, all said, just having fun.[10]

---

[1] The police took my BB gun and never returned it!

[2] Pretending to be from Hospital 1, I got blank birth certificates from Hospital 2.

[3] Sardines were the easiest.

[4] A giant Harley! My dream is still to run off with a '52 Vincent Black Lightning.

[5] Several nights in the central cellblock of the Halifax jail!

[6] Thank the Lord I was still a juvenile.

[7] This is the problem with my mom.

[8] Can you imagine having such a mom?

[9] The judge saw through to mom and me. Amazing woman, the judge that is.

[10] Life doesn't last long. You better have fun with it!

Please Don't Have My Funeral

Please don't have my funeral.
But if you must, leave me out of it.
I cannot bear even the thought.
Pew on pew only sparsely filled.
The minister at a loss officiating
for one so fallen from the faith.
My poor acquaintances
dragooned to speak,
struggling for a few nice words.
My last request songs totally
mismatched to the occasion.
People mulling about discussing
almost anything but me and
ready to get home for the ballgame.

I would have stayed alive
had I thought of all this!
Perhaps in lieu of flowers
and in lieu of anything else,
my friends, those remaining,
could gather and share thoughts
of the dumbest things I've said.
That would be fitting
as well as revealing and fun and
there is no shortage of material.

The Rhymer

There're many things that are a curse.
One of them, I found, is writing verse.
When painting, I saw shapes everywhere—
forms of bear and chair and curly hair.
With verse, a tumble of words float down.
One digs through them 'til the right one's found.
Then, it must stay still, well situated,
to see if a good rhyme germinated.

Some like me still believe in rhymes.
Some find rhymes as old as chimes.
Rhymes ... chimes, that works well.
Why not start with a good rhyme
and see what poem that foretells?

These random rhymes are from a book.
Can I use them with no gobbledygook?
Prayer – Despair
Surprise – Prize
Detest – Blessed
Resign – Design
OK, it's time now to have a look.

"The poet was near despair.
He felt he had not a prayer.
To losing, he was now resigned—
not the fate he once designed.
The judges he surely would detest.
But our poet was among the blessed.
The announcement was a big surprise.
His sassy poem had won first prize."

The Human Condition – Part III

I once knew an old couple
whose relationship was not very supple.
She was dreaming of new days
but he was set in old ways.
Just imagine the constant kerfuffle!

࿇

Fay was a person with miles to say.
Confidentiality was not in her DNA.
She was the local purveyor of gossip,
just like turning on the faucet,
until the day the hose aimed her way.

࿇

There once was an old man named Merv
whose ideas had been a bit ahead of the curve.
That gave him great hope.
Maybe he wasn't a dope.
His new views would soon hit a nerve.

There once was a man called Ray
who asked God what bills he should pay.
He found it was a great relief
to have such deep belief.
He was happy to his very last day.

∾

Erin was a woman of some daring.
At school she was already preparing.
She had something important in mind:
empowering those who were kind
and committed to neighborhood caring.

Leftovers

Truthiness: I will see it when I believe it.

Where does time go to die? To the Cuckoo's nest.

It's just a matter of time
        a splatter of wine
        a shatter of spine
        a clutter of crime
        a platter of lime
        a spatter of grime
        a blabber of mine

Maybe he will be younger by Election Day.

Rain, rein, reign,
please go away.
Maybe yet a poem,
but on another day.

The small strings vibrate.
It's subatomic music.
The quarks are singing.

I will rest my case
with the scarlet tanager.
There, in the plum tree.

The great Percy Bysshe Shelley said,
"Poets are the unacknowledged legislators of the world."
Today those words seem rather dead.
Still, they blaze across the banner here unfurled.
May these words be heard and not just read!

From the Author, a Word of Appreciation

I may be more surprised than you are that I have produced another book of poems and similar writings, my fifth. It surprises me also how quickly the year has passed since my last book, *The Blessings.* In any case, I hope you will enjoy this collection. Almost all these poems are new; a few have been incorporated from earlier books.

As you may know, I now have a personal website: www.gusspeth.org. Among other things, it contains a section with my complete poems from all five books: www.gusspeth.org/complete-poems. A collection of latecomers, found here in this volume, have not yet been added online.

To the certain embarrassment of some of them, I have named and thanked those who have helped me in my poetic efforts. I want to thank them again here, profusely, and praise their patience and good spirits: Cece Speth, Baron Wormser, E.B. Moore, Sam Love, Jennifer Brown, Karim Ahmed, David Grant, Sydney Lea, Ina Anderson, Catherine McCullough, Ethan Goffman, Mary Evelyn Tucker, John Grim, Richard Garcia, Jim Antal, Cindy Shannon, Jonathan Stableford, Byron Breese, Megan Mayhew Bergman, Pamela Harrison, Jim Speth, Charles Speth, Jenny Hane, Debbi Wraga, Chin Woon Ping, Tom Kinder, Carol Potter, John Keefe, and Clare Brant. Once again, as she did with my four previous poetry books, Anne Pace has done a marvelous job designing this presentation. You can see that.

The poet and novelist Baron Wormser recently wrote this about poetry: "Some formal dance is ever occurring in poetry. Urgency is forever making the acquaintance of reflection. ...Poetry has been as much a part of the tug and pull of modern times as any endeavor." These thoughts struck a chord with me.

I think my poems reflect my thoughts better than anything else I have written. Many of my favorites are in this volume.

Gus Speth
Strafford Vermont
Fall 2023

Printed in the USA
CPSIA information can be obtained
at www.ICGtesting.com
JSHW081108221123
52275JS00002B/7